HOW TO ROCK THE JOB INTERVIEW

CHAD STEWART

First published by Millennial Word Publications 2016
www.mwordpublications.com

Cover image taken from www.eduerf.net

❀ Created with Vellum

To Summer, my loving and supportive wife, who always sees more in me than I see in myself!

ACKNOWLEDGMENTS

I would like to thank my wife, Summer, who is always supportive of my many endeavours, and who never fails to offer sound advice and encouragement at the perfect times. I would also like to thank my friend and coworker, Jillian Macdonald, who meticulously went through the manuscript and offered her professional advice and critique which was invaluable. My boss, Brenda Nielsen, was additionally very positive and encouraging in the production of this work. Finally, I would like to thank the rest of my friends who reviewed the work before publication and put forth their views as to how to make it better.

1

PREFACE TO THE PREFACE!

Hi! So (Yes I know you're not supposed to start a sentence with the word "so" but this is my book and I don't care! *So* here it is!) you picked up this book because you want to get good (or better) at presenting yourself positively while being interviewed for a job. That's great! Before we get started, however, I would just like to lay it out there and tell you that I am not a Human Resources (HR) professional, have a Masters of Business Administration (MBA), nor am I in management anymore. How's that for pumping you up! Are you still with me? I don't pretend to have gone to business school, but the things you will learn in this book come from my experiences and a *perfect* track record of nailing job interviews for every job I had the skills and education for! How's that?

This book, then, as you will see, is a book of common sense. It contains straight up people skills, and a great working knowledge of the subject at hand. It is a book of the truth about my experiences over the last 20 years of my working life given to you (not totally free, but at a good cost I trust!). I have learned a few things through study and practice and would like to pass them on to you!

So (Yes I did it again!) hold on, sit back, and enjoy yourself! You're in for a ride!

PREFACE AFTER THE PREFACE TO THE PREFACE!

J oe looked at his watch in dismay as he sped through town looking for "Smith Brothers" machining company. He was at least five minutes late for his job interview and knew that this was not going to go over well with the people who were doing the hiring. For months he had tried to get an interview with this company, and now it had finally come but he could feel the possibility of a job with them slipping through his grasp.

Maybe I'll be able to talk my way out of being late like I always do, he thought as he pulled into the parking lot of "Smith Brothers".

The building was large and brown. It was shaped like a rectangle with a simple, large, sign hanging over the front entrance displaying the name of the company. It had a long walkway leading up to the front door and the grass around the building was cleanly landscaped. The few trees that dotted the property were of medium size and were well pruned. Along each side of the path leading to the front door stood rows of assorted flowers and shrubs.

Joe quickly parked his car, got out, and jogged up the

long path and into the building. Once inside he noticed a smiling secretary who greeted him warmly.

"I'm sorry I'm late," Joe stammered, embarrassed by his tardiness. "I have a job interview right now."

"That's ok," the secretary answered. "I'll let the managers and HR know you're here."

After a moment Joe noticed an older man, sharply dressed, walking toward him. The man smiled and held out his hand. "I'm Don," he said.

Joe, never being one for handshakes, grasped Don's hand limply and gave a light squeeze. "Nice to, um ... meet you," he said awkwardly.

Don smiled and said, "Please come this way."

The two walked down a short corridor and turned into the second doorway on the right. As they strolled down the hallway Joe remained quiet. The room they entered was well lit with a large oval table in the centre. As they entered Joe noticed two other people sitting at the table: a short stocky man with a round face, and a younger woman with shoulder length blonde hair. They both greeted him with smiles, handshakes, and introductions. The man's name was Devon, and the woman's name was Jennifer.

After the introductions were done, Don motioned for Joe to take a seat. Joe was positioned midway down the table with Jennifer on his right at the end, Devon across from Joe, and Don to his left at the other end.

After everyone was seated Devon asked Joe how he was doing.

"Good," replied Joe, looking down nervously and tapping his hand on his leg.

"Well ... " began Devon, "we have allotted thirty minutes for the interview. We have a number of what we call 'behavioural event' questions, where we will ask for specific examples as to a time you have demonstrated a certain behaviour. What you need to do is tell us what the situation was, how you handled it, and what the outcome was. Please try and be as specific as you can. We will all be asking questions and everyone will be taking notes. Don't be alarmed; it's for our benefit so we can remember how each candidate answers the particular question. We have bad memories." Devon smiled and chuckled as he ended.

Joe squirmed uneasily and tried to muster the best smile he could, but his stomach was so tied up in knots that even he didn't feel that his weak grin was anywhere close to sincere.

"Ok Joe," began Jennifer. "Can you please tell us a little bit about your previous work history ... say ... for the last five years?"

Joe swallowed hard and began to dictate his previous work history, which really wasn't too bad. His recitation of it, however, could have used some work. After he was done, Devon took the lead and asked the first question: "Who do you think is responsible for safety in the workplace, and why?"

Joe thought for a moment, and then said,

"The person who manages safety."

"Why do you believe that?" asked Devon. "Well ... I just think they are the ones who are getting paid for enforcing the rules"

"What about the workers themselves?" asked Don.

"Well I guess they should have an interest in it too," replied Joe, feeling a little like he blew this question because Don had to lead him on it.

"Can you tell us, Joe, have you ever seen a safety violation, and, if so, what did you do about it?" Devon asked.

Joe shuffled uncomfortably in his seat. "If I were to see

something that was unsafe I would immediately bring it to the attention of my manager."

Devon adjusted himself a little in his seat and stated, "What we are looking for is an actual example, from your own experience, of when you saw something unsafe and what, if anything, you did about it."

Awkward silence permeated the room for a moment, then Jennifer spoke up. "It doesn't have to be an example from work. What about in one of your hobbies, at home, or a family experience?"

Joe, again, was silent as he racked his brain for an example. He knew, in himself, that he has had scores of those experiences, but none of them came to mind at the moment. *Why didn't I prepare better for this?* He lamented in his head.

The interview lasted about twenty minutes and Joe left the premises feeling totally dejected and without hope of landing the job. This interview was nothing like he had expected. *Why was it so tough?* he asked himself.

THE SCENARIO above is similar to one that is played out in countless interviews across the world each and every day. In general, the working public are unfamiliar with the elements that make up a good interview presentation. As a manager of people myself, I knew first-hand that it is equally frustrating interviewing people who seem to know little, or nothing, about the interview process. What many fail to realize is that there are some basic elements that make up the job interview which, once mastered, will make it far easier to get the job you want; or at least make you a contender.

In the pages following, it is my hope that I will be able to enlighten you to those basic elements so you will be more successful in acquiring the job you are seeking. As I mentioned in the "Preface to the Preface" I write from experience as one who has not had difficulty presenting a good interview and getting the positions I was after. I am not perfect, but I managed to (as I mentioned before) get every job I was interviewed, and was qualified, for; I was 100% successful. I have interviewed nine times for jobs I had the skill-set for and have been successful in every one. This doesn't mean that everyone reading this book will be 100% successful after applying these principles. There are other factors involved in interviewing that you may have no way of impacting, such as: a conflicting personality with one of the hiring managers, or the fact that someone else had the same skill-set but the hiring team liked their examples better than yours, etc. This book does, however, give you a great understanding of the interview process and will allow you to present better if you understand the principles that are laid out in these pages.

At the beginning of my employment career I was not "locked into" what was making me successful; it was as I began to mature and move into positions of leadership when I realized what those elements were that I was doing which were making me "rock" the interviews. As a supervisor I was also given training which further unpacked and unlocked the interview process for me.

To further solidify the results I was experiencing, I had an opportunity to coach two of my firefighter friends (Yes, I am a firefighter as well!) in their interviews with two different major city fire departments. They were both successful. This was one of the experiences which inclined me to write this book and help others be more successful in their hunt for employment. The other experience which drove me to write this was my frustration as being the interviewer with people who have almost no concept of how to present themselves in an interview. Many, it would seem, do not understand what it takes to be the successful candidate for the jobs they are after. I think, also, that many of the ones who are successful have never really stopped to ask themselves why, but are naturally gifted in presenting themselves and pulling good answers to the questions from their experiences and presenting themselves well.

I believe that the principles I am going to present should be taught in every high school, and at every employment centre. Many good candidates have been passed by due to the outcome of their presentation in the interview. The outcome of the interview is something, to a fairly high extent, that everyone can positively impact by learning and practising these principles.

If you are one of those who has a great success rate, but have never understood why, this book will help you identify those reasons and, I hope, help you further perfect your skills. If you feel that you are inadequate at presenting yourself well in the interview, then I know this book will give you the skills you need if you put them into practice.

Let us journey together and begin to unlock the job interview process which will make you more successful in your hunt for the next employment opportunity.

3

FIRST IMPRESSIONS AND OTHER STUFF

The simple expression that "people look on the outside"; that is, that we make judgements by what we see, has been true since the dawn of time. As men and women, we can only use those external senses we were given to judge and assess the world around us, including other people. We can't read minds (If someone is talking to you in your head, that's not a good thing!), and we definitely can't sense someone's motives; all we can do is assess their actions, words, and body language. Everyone says that we shouldn't judge a book by its cover, but we do this all the time! Man! I can't tell you how many times I passed up on a book because the cover didn't appeal to me! I really hope the designer of this book didn't cheap out on its cover! Anyway ... back to the point. We do this because we are human. Even book marketers will tell you that you need to have a professional, sharp looking, cover if you want to attract people to pick up your book and at least look on the inside, hoping that they will like what they read as well.

Humans are the same everywhere you go, and this principle is as constant as the law of gravity. I would like to add, however, that what impresses one person may not impress another. The thought then is, that we need to present ourselves in such a way that is most likely to be noticed positively: we need to put ourselves in the most favourable position to influence the broadest section of people we can. There are certain generic principles, therefore, which we will discuss that have the maximum potential for positive first impressions.

I. Timeliness:

I have always been one who was concerned about being on time. In fact, I always try to be at least fifteen minutes early for appointments. Sometimes I leave too early and accidentally arrive thirty minutes before I need to! If this happens I will either wait in the car until ten or fifteen to, or go to the nearest coffee shop (if there is one around) and have a quick cup of coffee. There is a saying I learned at the fire department: "Ten minutes early is five minutes too late!" Of course, at the fire department, there is shift change which needs to take place, and a very real potential of getting a call right before the end of the shift of the firefighter you are there to relieve. Actually, when I do shifts at the fire department I will at times arrive thirty minutes early – over achieving on the expectation. The problem with this when going for a job interview is that you don't want to give the impression that you are too eager. This could give the managers a bad taste and set you back. I also find that waiting that long is almost unbearable.

I can't express how important this is. If you are ten to fifteen minutes early for your interviews, that immediately sets a positive image in the mind of the hiring manager. It speaks volumes regarding your personal character. It says that you are interested in what the company has to offer and are willing to sacrifice a little time in order to show them this. If, for whatever reason, you can't be on time make sure you call your potential employer and explain this to them, giving them the reason as to the delay. This shows that you are courteous; that you understand that their time is precious, and that you own up to possible mistakes on your part. Most managers and HR professionals will be gracious to this infraction and not hold it against you in the interview. All the same, it is best to be early.

II. Dress and Personal Image

Many people assume that if you are applying for a factory, construction, auto-mechanic, or any other labour or trade job that what you wear to the interview is unimportant. "Hey, it's not as though I'm looking for an office job," they reason.

To a certain extent they may have a point. I have interviewed lots of people for production/ manufacturing-type jobs where they have been successful even though their dress code would not have been considered anywhere close to business casual. But if you are the one who really wants to do all the right things in order to give yourself the best shot, then your clothes and personal image play an important role.

The view I take is that you should do everything within your power to look, act, and feel professional even if you are not applying for a professional/office position. You should try to exceed the expectations of the norm. The actor Jonny Depp has made a reputation for himself of going over and above any expectations others may have of the roles he plays. He is, quite truthfully, one of the best actors of our time. The way he does this is by doing all that he can and then giving it that little bit extra. This principle should hold true in any endeavour we take in life. It certainly holds true in the realm of job interviews. Despite the fact that we can probably get a job without necessarily holding ourselves to a high standard of dress code, we ought to strive for that next level and attempt to separate ourselves from the rest of the pack.

I was impressed by one of our production assemblers where I work because every time he was interviewing for a different job within the plant he would ensure that he changed into a collared shirt and tie for the interview! He knew this principle and lived it!

What kind of dress code is acceptable? This is a loaded question, and I am sure there are many employment experts around the world who would love to weigh in at this point. I would like to say at the outset that I'm not going to tell you exactly what to wear. Instead, I will point out some general principles that should make it easy for everyone to dress appropriately for the interview process.

Principle #1: Business or Business Casual?

I would like to repeat my earlier statement that it does not matter what type of job you are applying for, you should dress in such a way that your appearance is professional and sharp. The easiest way to dress in this manner is to dress in what we call business or business casual. For men, what this means for business casual is a nice pair of pants (dress or khakis), collared shirt, and dress shoes. If you prefer going with the full-on business look you should also add a matching suit jacket and tie.

For women, this can be a nice dress, or a skirt and blouse; you may even have a nice sweater that would make a good addition over top of the blouse. If you ladies would like to step it up a notch you can always go with the full-on business suit. Remember, you always want to portray a professional image, so do yourself a favour and do not allow any cleavage to be showing; this is not the way you want to attempt laying hold of a job! You want to appear professional, courteous, and sharp.

Principle #2: Cleanly Cut

The idea behind being cleanly cut is *not* that you necessarily have to be clean shaven and have a short hair cut; the principle is broader than that. What I mean is that you can have a beard, or longer hair, and still be considered cleanly cut. It means that your hair is done nicely and your beard (if you have one) is well trimmed and taken care of. For women, your hair should be done nicely (you don't have to go to extremes and have a full makeover!), in order to show that you take care of yourself and are interested in making a good first appearance. Some women always wear a bit of makeup, which is fine. Just don't overdo it. My wife never wears makeup and looks awesome!

At our company we had, at one time, a rather interesting process for bringing people in for interviews. What we did was first scrutinize the resumes and then decide who we would like to bring in for, what we call, a "meet and greet." At this meet and greet we got to see, first hand, the actual people that were behind the paper on the resume. We had a brief talk about our company: who we are, what we do, and what we can offer. We then had a plant tour and, after that, would bring them back for a round table discussion about what each of their history was: work experience, education, etc. After this, they would fill out a form which explained what they liked about the company and how they believed they could be a fit in our organization. The hiring managers, who were introduced and had a part in discussing the open positions we had to offer, would then leave and decide who out of the group they are interested in bringing in for an interview. Only those individuals were contacted.

You may be asking: "What does this have to do with

being cleanly cut?" That's a good question. The reason I bring this up is because at one of our meet and greets there was a young man, James, who seemed to be sharp and had the skills we were looking for. At the meet and greet he had shoulder length hair (that seemed un-kept) and a fairly scruffy beard, but because he had the skill-set we were looking for we invited him for an interview. When he came for the interview, however, his hair was cut short, neatly brushed, and he had shaved his beard; I almost didn't recognize him. The point is that this simple act impressed us. It showed us a guy who was serious about being hired on. He was serious enough to update or improve his look!

Principle #3: Limit the Cologne/Perfume

It's surprising to note that there are a lot of people out there that either, can't handle the smell of cologne and perfume, or don't like the smell of certain fragrances. I remember one time when I came in for a shift at the fire department that I had put on my normal cologne that morning and didn't think anything more of it. I had actually received quite a few remarks in the past as to how nice it smelled, but that morning there was a firefighter just getting off shift who asked which of us in the oncoming crew was wearing cologne because he said it was really powerful. He further remarked that if we were dealing with any medical situations that day it may not go so well with the patients.

I didn't think I had put on more that morning than normal, but apparently this guy was really sensitive to it! It was a really good lesson for me because I realized that I should be sensitive to the fact that not everyone is going to appreciate the fragrance. I determined from that point on to either not wear it on shift, or tone it down so as not to be potentially offensive. I think the same idea can be utilized in the interview process. If you are planning on wearing cologne or perfume, then just remember to use it lightly. I personally like the smell of many different types of perfume, but just remember that not everyone is like me.

III. Initial Greeting

When you first greet someone this is one of the best times to make a great first impression. This part of the meeting, therefore, is very critical. Some people are naturally sociable which makes this very easy and comfortable to manage; they seem to be able to converse with people very easily wherever they go. For those who are not like this you may need to practice meeting people.

I know from my own experience that I was always very sociable around those I got to know well, but I used to feel awkward around strangers and very self conscious. For those who know me now and not back then, they may find this very shocking given the fact that I am now fairly conversant with almost anyone I am around; I no longer have problems meeting people and making a decent first impression most of the time (no one is 100% on their game all the time!).

How did I develop this? The same way I managed to develop any of the skills I have acquired: learning and practice. I found out that the more I learned about people, and put myself "out there" to meet others, the easier it became. It's like anything in life: the more you practice the better you will be.

Principle #1: Smile

When I was about fourteen years old I was incredibly self conscious of my looks. It seemed as though none of my clothes fit me properly, I was the shortest kid in my class, I was probably 100 pounds soaking wet, and I could never determine which way my hair wanted itself to be brushed! To top it off, I spent the previous two years coping with a massive case of acne. Those commercials they have on about acne make me laugh! I watch them and think, "This girl has an issue? She has one zit and *her* life is over?! I have literally hundreds!" Seriously, my face looked like a pizza! Talk about issues because, as we all know, kids can be cruel, especially in junior high! Well, that was my life, until one day I met a girl named Sarah.

Sarah was probably the most beautiful girl I had met up to this point in my life. She wasn't "knock-out model-type" attractive, but rather had a cute look with blonde hair, deep brown eyes, and a really nice smile. Her personality was very pleasant and charming. For whatever reason (and I can't seem to remember that well) my friends and I began hanging around her and some of her friends. While on recess one day, when we were all hanging out at a table in the library and joking back and forth, Sarah turned to me out of the blue and said, "Chad, you have a really nice smile. You should show it more often." BANG! Instantly my life was transformed by that simple statement! I felt, up to that point, that I really had no redeeming qualities. But there it was, Sarah liked my smile!

From that moment on, I determined to smile as often as I could and I actually began to develop my sense of humour. Everywhere I looked from then on, I noticed that *everyone* had a nice smile; that is, if it is sincere and not mischievous. Let me explain. If you know that someone is smiling or laughing at the expenses of others, or due to some evil intent, it turns what was supposed to be nice into a fraud. Looking objectively, however, if you just saw a picture of someone smiling and you did not know why, you would have to conclude, probably most of the time, that they really do have a nice smile.

This, in my experience, is a universal principle. Now I

know that there are some people who will reject this thought and say, "What about the 98-year-old woman over there with one tooth, or the man over there with the smashed in face due to an accident? You can't tell me that their smiles are nice." Well, if that's the way you think then maybe you need an attitude check? I personally like every sincere smile I see. Then there are those of you out there who will tell me that I am too idealistic and optimistic. To that charge I say: "I don't care." How's that for a response?

I'm telling you, don't go into an interview appearing morose and somber. On the other hand, all things need to tempered and done in moderation. In other words, don't go into an interview "flying off the wall" with enthusiasm either! They may think you've just landed from another planet! Or, you're about to shoot them all!

Be pleasant. Smile sincerely.

Principle #2: Firm Handshake

At this point you may be saying to yourself: "Come on, is it really necessary to be getting into these common, socially acceptable, practices? These are basic civilities that everyone knows!" Well let me ask the question: "*Does* everyone know these 'basic civilities'?" In my experience it surprises me to see how many people actually do not know the proper way to handshake. Or that a smile goes a long way. This is why I am including this brief information here. If you already know these social practices, then by all means skip this section. For the sake of thoroughness, however, I felt the need to add these elements here.

When meeting with people for the first time the initial handshake is very important. Think back if you can with me for a moment. Each of us, to this point (wherever you are in life), must have shaken hands with multitudes of people already. Now you probably have had the unfortunate circumstance of being involved in what I call a PEH (poorly executed handshake). You might have even been the cause!

So here it is. It's a beautiful day and everything seems to be normal (relative to your life of course) and you're with a friend who is introducing you to another friend, relative, close acquaintance, etc. and you start to go in for the handshake. Everything seems normal. Your hands are coming closer and closer. Fingers are appropriately spaced. Height is good. Speed seems fine. Your hands are getting closer and closer. You're both smiling and making eye contact. You glance down for a moment to ensure a lock with the other person's hand. Then it happens! One of you closes too early and now you both feel that instead of a handshake you should be turning the person's hand and giving them a kiss on the back of it like was done in times past when greeting a lady in society! *Why did this have to happen?* you scream to yourself (in your head of course!). Everything was going so well! Was it me who closed too early or them? You don't know because by this time you are in such a daze that all you want to do is retract from this disgraceful performance of a handshake (PEH)!

Or maybe instead of this kind of poorly executed handshake you have run into people who feel it is their duty in life to dominate you with the alpha dog handshake crush of doom! I've heard this is actually a wrestling move, but I have yet to verify the validity of this claim. You all know what I'm talking about. This is the handshake that is too powerful, too dominating, too aggressive. When you shake this person's hand it is as though your hand has been securely placed in a vice that rivals the torture machines used during the Spanish inquisition!

Or how about the time you went to grasp someone's hand and you wondered if they just had a stroke in front of you because there was barely any pressure when they close, thus giving you the impression you were shaking a limp noodle!

Of course all of this is an overly dramatic representation of things to avoid, but I think these illustrations help drive my point home nicely. You need to avoid the extremes of the "early closure," "grip of doom," or "limp noodle."

I would also like to add that, if you are a sweater when you get nervous and sweat is gushing out of every pour of your hands, then asked politely to be excused from the handshake as your hands are perspiring. This is easy to do. Just say something like this: "Sorry, but I'd rather not shake as my hands are pretty sweaty right now and I don't think it would be a good experience for you." Whomever you are shaking hands with will respect that and give you leeway for not shaking.

The proper handshake needs to have full closure with a firm (but not over powering) squeeze. If you recognize that you are one of these individuals that do not perform the handshake well, then my recommendation to you is to practice; you will get better. What if you are not the one who transgresses in the execution of the handshake? Don't stress out over it, it happens. Just smile and make eye contact and you will be ok. Or, you can always use it as a joke and decry, "Oh no! We just had a PEH!" At this point the people will look at you weirdly, at which time you can explain the "Poorly Executed Handshake" and apologize for your part in the tragedy! Another technique I learned from a friend of mine a while ago was that, if this happens to you, you can always grab the person's arm at the elbow with your other hand and gently put your hands together in the proper position and smile.

The last thing I would like to add before we move on is

that you need to ensure that you make eye contact when you shake someone's hand. This will display confidence in your greeting and will work to set things in a positive light when you meet people.

Principle #3: Introduction

When you introduce yourself try to make sure you are clear and articulate, or at least as clear as you can be. I know that some people have a natural way of talking that may not be as clear as others; most people will understand that this is probably normal for you upon your first meeting. If you have a natural disposition to mumble, then it's not the end of the world, because, with practice, you can overcome this. Believe me, I know, because I had the worst mumble ever! In fact, sometimes it still comes back to haunt me on occasion. There are moments when I need to consciously think about being clear in order to overcome my natural inability. If I can do it, then so can you! Remember, most managers are professional people who have seen countless personalities and styles of interaction and can understand in a moment roughly where you fit in on the grid they have in their mind. Oh yes, they have had enough experiences with people (as they are "Managers of People") that they will start to assess you right away as soon as they see you. Don't panic! They are people too who also fit in with the "grid of society" and have learned that numerous "styles of people" (if I can say it that way) can be a definite asset to their organizations. Usually they will not judge you too harshly until they are fully into the interview process. It is at this point that they will begin making their judgements as you answer the questions they have for you. But we will talk about the question portion later in detail.

Hopefully I haven't scared too many of you away at this point! Judgment calls in social circumstances, however, are a natural part of human interaction; everyone makes these judgement calls differently, based on their own personalities. What you need to do, is to make sure that you can appeal to the broadest cross-section of human interaction when you meet with people, and bring them to the point where the managers are making objective decisions based on your fit for their organization.

What! You're thinking! I thought we weren't supposed to judge people! This is a common misconception in our world as modern society , or culture, doesn't think deeply about their own lives to consider what they are saying. Everyone makes judgement calls everyday! If you don't make judgement calls then you're either: 1) not a person, or 2) dead! Let me ask you: "How do you decide what to wear in the morning? Or what to eat for breakfast, or even if you have breakfast? How about deciding what people to make as your close friends and which ones to keep at arms length because they may not be a good fit for you and you know this? How do you decide what political party to vote for if you don't make "judgments?" Let's be honest: we all make judgement calls.

Ok, let's take this a step further when dealing with people. How many of you have ever worked with someone who, for whatever reason, refuses to use arm deodorant or body spray? You're making a judgement in your mind whether or not you like that! Most people don't. The person may be perfectly nice and you interact with them on that level, but you try and limit your closeness to them because of their odour. That's naturally human to do and this rose-coloured glasses idea about not making judgement calls is complete tripe! (Yes, I just used a British expression! Why? Because I wanted to!) My wife works in the school system as a Special Educational Assistant and she works with some kids who don't shower (or their parents don't make them shower) and she says that, because of this, they tend to get less teacher time! Does that sound harsh? Unfortunately, it's natural and we need to accept that aspect of society. If you don't accept and understand this, then you will limit yourself and your opportunities. I always tell my kids that it's a game, and they need to play the game. If you smell so strong during an interview it may be such a distraction that you are literally hindering yourself. You have become your own worst enemy!

Wow! You might be thinking: "That's a lot to process!" Don't tie yourself into knots about it. As you continue to develop (if you haven't already) the generally accepted social norms of interview interaction these abilities will come natural. Trust me!

After the introduction it's always ok to start with some "small talk." The manager or HR might even start off this kind of conversation. Remember, they are supposed to be human experts (or at least know enough to be good at this!) and they will probably try and put you at ease. They understand that interviews can be stressful for some people and even managers have a heart and some sensibility about them. Or at least most do! Some, unfortunately, can't be helped and got into management positions because they possess a degree and have absolutely no idea how to deal with people! I'd like to think that this group is a minority, but I could tell you some stories that would have you shaking your head and wondering what possessed some companies into hiring managers who don't know the first thing about how to treat people, even though they just got the high responsibility of managing people! Anyway ... I digress. Sorry about that. Let's get back to the point.

The small talk is really just an icebreaker in order for the manager(s), HR, and the prospective employee a brief time in order to size each other up. This, again, is not bad, it's just human nature. This happens every time you meet someone new. Most people have lots of experience with this so it should not bother you. If you are naturally recluse and awkward, however, (because there are some out there who are, and it's perfectly natural for them) don't worry; it just means that you need to practice this a little before you go to the interview. You may need to have a friend or family member help you with your handshake and small talk.

The small talk usually focusses around the weather, your drive in, how your day's going, etc. These are everyday questions and conversations that everyone has from time-to-time. Relax. It's ok. Just make sure that you don't overdo it as you try to make a good first impression.

A typical conversation might go like this: "Hi, my name is Sofia Brown."

"Hi Sofia. I'm Lydia Cross. How are you today?"

"Not bad. The weather's decent and I was able to find this place without getting too lost." "Well that's definitely a bonus!"

"How's your day so far Lydia?"

"Not bad. It's been pretty steady around here which is always a good thing in a down economy."

"Definitely!"

You get the idea? It's not rocket science, just human science! The more you can develop these skills the better your chances will be. And remember: The mistakes we make are learning experiences which make us better for the next go- around!

IV. Detailed Introduction

After you have been introduced to everyone who will be interviewing you, they will usually ask you to explain a little bit about yourself. This is an important step as they are sizing you up and seeing if you are a relatively normal person. You might think that this is a strange way of explaining it, but believe me, some people have said things in interviews at this point that just make you wonder what they were thinking. And then you realize that, for your own sanity, you don't want to know what they were thinking!

For example, during one interview I was conducting with some other managers the girl we were interviewing told us that she was having a rough time with her ex-boyfriend. In fact, he apparently tied her up, threw her in his trunk, and drove to a different city with her! She somehow got away and was able to make it back home. I'm not making this stuff up!

On another occasion a young man revealed to us at this stage that he was part of a heavy metal rock back that played gigs once in a while and asked if I would like a free copy of his CD to listen to. It's too bad for him that I don't listen to heavy metal.

The point is that you need to stay away from the stuff that sounds weird. It may have happened to you, but your prospective managers don't need to know it!

There are four simple points that make this step a piece of cake if you apply them consistently.

Principle # 1: Be honest

Be honest about who you are in general. Treat this the same way you would if you were meeting someone for the first time and they asked you a couple of simple questions about who you are. You don't have to fabricate stories to make yourself more interesting.

I once worked with a guy that would make up the most ridiculous stories and tell them to you as though they were fact! Even when he was challenged to the validity of the stories he wouldn't back down. He told us that the cops once shut down the highway between Calgary and Edmonton in order to let him race a brand new sports car. He also, apparently, helped JFK found the navy seals, which was really interesting given the fact that he was maybe 20 years older than me at the time and this story was told to us about 1999. He also apparently saved the governor of Colorado's granddaughter from terrorists and was awarded a million dollars! At the time he told this he was living in a single-wide mobile home in a small town in Alberta. It went on and on! The funny thing was that this guy actually did do some cool stuff in life but he never spoke about it. He was actually an actor with a small bit part on a TV series that was filmed around the Calgary area in the 90's. Maybe this wasn't cool enough I guess, but how many people do you know that are actors, even for small parts?

People appreciate honesty and integrity and this should come out in the interview. Most managers have a really good sense of people and can spot a fraud just by conversing with them for a while. I call this managerial sixth sense. I have literally sat in interviews with other really experienced managers and, after all is said and done, they say that there is something wrong with that person but they can't put their finger on it. There was something the candidate said, or the way he said it, that triggered them that there was something off. Then again, no one is perfect and we have all been fooled from time to time. I remember a few times when I got that nagging feeling but played it off as being too sensitive, or having gas or indigestion, only to realize when the person started that I made a horrible mistake!

I'm going to go out on a limb and say that probably 99.9% of the people reading this book are not like this. I bet you all just want to get better at interviewing because you need help. Very few people seem to teach this skill, and the ones who are really successful at it are those who have a natural talent for it.

Principle #2: Be concise

You don't need to explain everything about yourself or what you have done. You just need to give them enough so they can get to know you a bit. This can be hard when you're in a pressure situation such as an interview, as it's easy for people to ramble on due to being nervous. If your interviewers want more information than they'll ask. This principle can be illustrated by that scene in the movie "Goonies" where the bad guys capture the kid, Chunk, and ask him to tell them "all he knows" (obviously about the treasure they were after), and Chunk starts reiterating his entire childhood! In my EMT (Emergency Medical Technician) training they were specific when they instructed us to make sure, when dealing with a geriatric patient, to ask specific questions about *relevant* past medical history. If you don't, you will be in for a long list of ailments, most of which are *not* relevant!

Principle #3: Be positive

It's ok to smile and be enthusiastic when telling someone about yourself; just don't overdo it. It's ok to let them know that you appreciate the opportunity of having the interview. Some of you may have to work at this aspect a little. I know that there are personality types out there that aren't the most outgoing or positive. This isn't a bad thing; it's just a fact. You may be wired differently and will have to work at portraying some moderate positivity. Don't let your natural personality get the better of you because you aren't inclined to as much social interaction as others. It just means that you may have to work harder at it. I'm not naturally inclined to exhibiting patience; it's something I have been working on for a while and will probably continue to work on it for the rest of my life. I've gotten way better, but I'm still not where I want to be. I have also had to develop more logical thinking through the years because that just does not come natural to me. I've grown in leaps and bounds in that area too, but I've had to work at it. It's just who I am. Many think that I'm a natural-born leader, but that too is not accurate. I have learned and honed those skills throughout years of study and experience. If you're not inclined to a cheery disposition or positivity, then maybe that's something you should consider consciously developing.

The Conclusion to the Matter:

Mastering this information won't mean that you will nail every interview you have, but it will definitely put the odds in your favour. You need to make sure that the deck is stacked! To do this you need to do everything you can to make a great first impression. And by all means, take from this what will work for you and throw out the rest. If you use the knowledge of human nature to work for you, not against you, you will see greater success, and it will be awesome!

As was stated in The Hunger Games: "May the odds ever be in your favour." This will be true because you have studied, changed, practiced, and grown your ability.

4

THE INFAMOUS QUESTION STYLE

W e now enter the part of the interview process that many people struggle with: the interview questions. This, however, is probably the most important part of the process! Some people seem to just have a natural way about themselves which makes this experience fairly stress-free and easy to overcome. Others, however, have major anxiety during this time. It's almost like having test anxiety. I know that some of you who are reading this can definitely relate. Before the big test your mind is consumed with anxiety about passing, what kind of questions will be asked, did you study enough, if you fail you will have to take the class again or it will make your mark plummet, etc., etc., etc. Having a little bit of worry is ok as it should have propelled you earlier to study harder, but major anxiety will only hurt you. I find that the best way to deal with anxiety is to ensure that you have studied and practiced hard enough so that you are confident that you will be able to pass. In other words: you are prepared to take the test or interview.

I'm one of those ones who really never had any problems answering the questions the way they wanted them answered, which is the main reason why I have been so successful in nailing down jobs. The truth of the matter is that there is nothing to be worried about if you prepare properly. Not everyone can think on their feet; some may need a little more preparation. This section is, therefore, designed to give you the basic idea of the philosophy, format, and the overall structure behind the modern interview style. This information will help you to have an understanding as to why the interviewers ask the questions they do.

I. The Philosophy

There is a very simple design to the modern interview which makes a lot of sense if you think it through. The philosophy of choosing the right person begins with the basic idea that *past history is the best determiner of future action*. What the heck does that mean?! It's very simple really. They (Don't ask me who the "they" is! This is the mystical ethereal "they" you always hear about when no one knows who really developed something! I'm sure there is a history of this you can research to find these answers, but I just don't think its very important right now!) have determined (in general) that a person's actions in a certain situation which he performed in the past will be a pretty good indication of what he will do in the future.

Now, I just want to throw out a little disclaimer at this point and say that this is not always the case. Why, you ask? Because we're human! And humans have a tendency of being inconsistent once in a while. Even the most consistent person in the world is inconsistent at times! Did I just blow your mind, or what! This inconsistency, in my experience as a human and observing other humans around me, can be occasioned by environmental pressures, circumstances, physical or mental wellness, personal life stressors, etc. The reason I make this statement is to guard my butt, just in case any of you are in management (or end up in management) and you have a person you hired do exactly the opposite in a situation then what he said in the interview! The first thing you'll say is: "Man, Chad was totally wrong about this process and led me down a dark path of no return and now I have a dud for an employee! What a jerk!"

If this happens to you, please see aforesaid disclaimer and get off my back! I mean that in the best possible way.

Now, where were we? Oh yeah, talking about the philosophy that drives this thing. As I was saying, the history of a person's actions is important. This is why, as we will see later in the book, the questions they ask in this type of interview are *specific*. The interviewers will actually ask for specific examples of real life situations that you have had that fit a general theme of a quality they are checking out in you. A lot of people are not used to this type of questioning and are hard pressed to come up with a specific example at the time, even though the situation may have happened to them multiple times.

It was really sad one time when a manager friend of mine and I were conducting an interview with a 19-year-old who had worked a little with us over the summer but now wanted a full time position that was posted. He clearly did not understand at all what we were asking. Every time we asked if he could give a real example of a certain situation he would respond by saying: "If that happened to me than this is what I would do." Unfortunately, he was unable to give real life examples even though I knew that he probably had ones he could use. After a while my friend started trying to coax more out of him and lead him a little (something managers are not supposed to do!) because she felt so bad for him, seeing him flounder like a fish out of water, gasping for every breath until he finally died. He didn't really die though! I just wanted to clarify that before I gave you the wrong idea! We did not kill anyone! But I digress.

She actually told me after that she felt so bad, her mothering instincts started to kick in and she was literally trying to spoon-feed him into making his answers more meaningful. We both felt so bad for him. A few months later I met him at Tim Hortons as I was standing in line to buy a coffee. I asked how he was doing and he said fine. He then asked me what I had against him and why I wouldn't hire him. He said he was a hard worker and he could do the job. So I tried to explain to him again that his interview wasn't good because he couldn't give us any information as to how he actually handled himself in previous employment, school, or just in his personal life. I told him that we did everything we could to give him a chance (in fact this was the second interview we provided for him as we tried to help him out) and that we just couldn't justify offering the position to him over other candidates who had better interviews. I suggested that he learn more about the interview process and told him that I hoped he was able to succeed. I don't think he heard a word I said as he went away angry.

Actually, this experience is another one of the main reasons why I was convicted to write this book. I felt so bad for him because he just didn't understand this vital process in job acquisition. He needs some training, and I wager there are many other people out there who need this training as well.

Some have given this idea of past history predicting future action a fancy acronym: STAR. This stands for: Situation, Task, Action, Result. They even call this a "Behavioural Interview Technique!" Doesn't that sound fancy?! It must be awesome! Actually, it does work quite well and I will show you why and how in the coming pages. I will show you how to be a "STAR" in the interviewing process!

II. The Format

Oops! I just let the cat out of the bag before you got to this section what the format is. It's simple to remember. And I'll show you later that it's also simple to apply. All you have to remember is STAR! (Situation, Task, Action, Result) That's it!

So how does this work? It's very simple really. Those who are conducting the interview are going to ask very specific questions (which I will cover examples of in a later section). These questions, as I stated above, are designed to first, see what situations you have encountered in past experience; secondly, to see how you handled it; and thirdly, see what resulted from the action you took which brought about a favourable result. There are also some questions, however, which are designed to bring out how you failed at handling a situation (let's face it, we can't always be rock stars! At least I can't!) in order to see how you reacted to that failure, but I'll talk about that later.

It was a real eye-opener to me when I began conducting interviews as to how many people had trouble navigating this style of questioning. For some reason it just came natural to me. They always asked me for a specific time and example that demonstrated a specific skill/ability which they were looking for. Now, I get that sometimes it's hard to come up with a situation off- the-cuff which can make this style of interview frightening to some people, but I will talk later about how to handle that so you can be successful during the interview process.

III. The Overall Structure

The last idea of this point is to learn more about the

overall structure. Everything we said above is speaking to this aspect in some way or another, but this really ties it all together. So if you look at the purpose and reason that the interview is structured this way, you really start to understand the questions they ask and the reason they ask them. What I mean is that the structure of this process is such that it allows the hiring managers to get to know you and your work habits, shall we say, a little better in order for them to judge whether or not you're a good fit for their organization. The overall structure, therefore, they have chosen to unlock this information is seen in the way the behavioural interview takes shape from beginning to end. The whole interview has been designed to allow them to make the best possible decision with the available data that is before them.

When I use the term "overall structure" then, I mean the way in which the interview is conducted. Before the questioning begins they may tell you that they are going to be taking notes of the things you say in your answer to the questions. They usually tell you this so that you will not be overwhelmed or nervous with their scrawling. It's a point of courtesy. This was illustrated at the beginning in the narrative I wrote about Joe going for an interview at "Smith Brothers." Now, just to note: some managers write more than others. Do not be psyched out or read anything into this! Some managers just like to write more than others. The notes really help them to remember the interview afterwards, because when they are flipping through their possible choices of interviewees for the job, things they have written will trigger them to remember the specific person easier. Some interviewing forms even have a numbering/rating system that helps them see who scored higher than others. This rating system is completely subjective from one person to the next, but it helps that hiring manager bring forward the individuals he or she liked, and the ones that they felt did not do very well.

The thing to remember here is that the overall structure for this process is systematic. The questions are always predesigned for the particular business, and many times for the particular positions which are up for grabs. The questions, therefore, will make sense as they usually progress is a logical order. There will be more about this later.

Having a working knowledge of why and how this whole interview process is put together is half the battle. Like they used to say in one of the best 80's and 90's cartoons they ever made, GI Joe: "Knowing is half the battle!"

"Go Joe!"

5

HOW TO ANSWER AND THEREFORE
IMPLIED HOW NOT TO ANSWER

This is the part where things really start to get exciting! I know all of you are sitting on the edge of your seats just waiting for me to unlock the power and scream with HE MAN: "I have the powerrrrr!" Yes, this is another reference to an 80's cartoon series that was pretty awesome.

Seriously though, I will say at the outset that there is not a hard and fast, clinical, robotic- type answer that you can use for every interview and every question as every interview is different and the questions will be different too. I will say, however, that there are specific principles that can be used for every question that should help you through the minefield relatively unscathed.

In fact, there are three simple points I would like to make in this section that will dramatically improve your chances in the behavioural interview. And yes, they are put down using Roman Numerals. As you have already guessed: I like Roman Numerals! The modern age seems to be against them as they are hard to come across nowadays, but seriously: what harm have they done to anyone?!

I. Take your time

I told you these were going to be life- altering! Remember, usually you only have one crack to make a good first impression and you can't be rushing into this thing like a bull in a china shop on steroids! You need to show that you are thoughtful about the questions they are asking you, and that you really are attentive in trying to pull from the best example you can think of.

I always tell people that awkward silence is ok in a job interview. What do I mean by that? Well, let's say they ask you a question and you know you have an example, but you just can't quite remember it, or the specific details. It's ok to say something like this: "That's a tough question. Do you mind if I think about it for a minute?" Or, "Wow, that's a good question. I know this has happened to me before. Do you mind if I have a minute to remember the details of the situation?" After you say this, feel free to let the seconds tick by while you remember the details of your circumstance. Managers don't mind. A little word of caution, however: don't take too long. There is such a thing as awkward silence and then there is *annoying* silence! Make sure you don't drift into the latter kind!

The reason that this kind of awkward silence is expected by hiring managers is because they know that people sometimes need time to fire up their memory in order to provide the best possible example they can. This is commonplace. When the silence becomes annoying is when it lasts for an unusual length of time. What length of time is that? You ask. I don't know. Unfortunately, this is something that you need to judge for yourself. It's not a scientific piece of data, but rather, more of a gut feel. You will know when the awkward becomes annoying. If this happens and you still don't have an answer then just say to the managers that you can't think of a specific circumstance right now and you would like to circle back to this question later. Most managers will consent to the request and move on to the next question. You need to make sure, however, that you don't do this again on any of the following questions as it will make you appear incompetent. You usually only get one lifeline. Thankfully, if you prepare properly, you will not have to use this option in most of the interviews you attend. I just wanted to let you know that it is here if you need it. And, just to ease your concern about this, I have used this lifeline in one interview before and was still hired for the position; so it does work!

II. Be Specific

If you remember the philosophy I detailed above that past experience is a good indicator of future action, then you will have to agree that a specific answer is far better than a vague one. I don't know how many interviews I have been involved in as the hiring manager where the candidate was so vague and uncommitted with his answer. As a manager you really need the candidate to throw you a bone! It's hard to make a good decision when you have very little to go off of! If you want to, therefore, secure the position you are after (or at least give it your best shot!) then you must give them what they need. And what they need is your best (if you can remember it) situation, including the task that was assigned or that you saw needed to be addressed, your actions, and the resultant outcomes that came from your actions. It's really quite simple with a bit of practice and thought.

As way of a side note, I also want to point out that there are vast companies (mostly smaller ones) who don't use this format and are content with the old way of interviewing. These people usually don't ask for specific situations in their questioning format. If you run into one of these styles of interviews, then my suggestion to you is to use this format anyway! The reason I say that is because this way of interviewing is, in my opinion, far superior to anything else I have seen. Let me give you an example.

Let's say you are in an interview for a manufacturing job and the hiring manager asks: "Is health and safety important to you?" (Wow! You'd have to braindead to say no! Duh!) But instead of just that, you say, "Yes, of course it is. I remember one time in a previous job making ... , that we received steel into the plant that looked as though it was on a larger skid than normal. So I went over to check the weight on the skid before the operator lifted it with the forklift and sure enough our lift didn't have the capacity in order to move the load safely. Because of this I did ..." Isn't that a lot better than, "Man! Do I ever love safety! It is my life! I am one of the safest people I know! They actually called me Mr. Safety at my last job! In fact, my picture has been featured on cereal boxes because of my superhero safety?!"

Specifics, specifics, specifics! It shows them that, even though you say you are a safety conscious person, you have actually backed it up with down-to-earth true experiences that you have had. An HR friend of mine says that, as soon as she hears the word "we" when someone is answering one of these questions, her ears turn off! She wants to know what *you* have done *specifically* in this circumstance!

III. Answer Honestly

This point should be a no-brainer to people! Honesty and integrity are elements of personal character that are admired. I know there is a general feeling that everyone loves someone who's on the edge and daring, but my main point is that you can be courageous and daring with personal integrity. If you asked people today who they like more, Iron Man or Captain America, most will invariably pick Iron Man; usually because he's a rebel. Again, if you ask people if they like

Deadpool or Captain America more, it's frightening how many people say Deadpool! Personally I think he's a jerk with no integrity! (Yes, this is another one of my sidetracks!) The point is, however, that it's hard to speak derogatorily about someone who is a stand-up person with a clear sense of direction and honesty. People may like Iron Man or Deadpool more than Cap, but they can never fault Cap on his integrity and character!

When answering the questions that are put to you do NOT fabricate a circumstance! I say again. Do NOT fabricate a situation in order to impress your perspective employers. This will only turn out bad in the end. Be as honest as you can; they appreciate that. Remember, most things you say can be verified in a reference check!

I know you might be a little vague on the details of the situation you are trying to remember from a while ago, but that's ok. Let them know you're having trouble remembering the specifics and that you can only give them the sense of the situation. Just make sure your actions and results are presented as clearly as you can remember them. If you do that you'll be ok.

Taking your time, being specific, and being honest are simple but powerful techniques that will benefit you in your quest for the next job.

6

SPECIFIC EXAMPLES TO NAIL IT!

I t was a dark and stormy night! The wind blew through the trees rustling their branches. Leaves broke free from their perch upon those very branches which gave them their sustenance. You walk along the path with the sense that a thousand eyes are upon you, peering into your soul, and almost driving you mad with the anticipation that at any moment someone, or something, is about to leap from the shadows and throttle you!

You sense movement to your right and glance over to see nothing but the dark shape of the trees swaying in the wind. Then, from the other side, something takes hold of you! Instinctively, you reach around and find that it is a strong hand grabbing you roughly! From the body language, you know that the person holding you is not doing so for your good, but rather your harm. Instead of panic, however, you feel a sense of confidence. You know that there is a good chance that this person is not a match for you as you have trained in hand-to- hand combat since you were a child, have been in countless battles before, and have honed your body and mind into a fighting machine!

Quickly, before the person has a chance, you move almost purely by instinct and grab the attackers hand, twisting it around in an awkward position. With lightning speed, you knife-hand thrust your opponent in the throat and the battle is over. Your attacker is now face down in the mud holding his throat, regretting that he ever tried to harm you; for it is as some say in karate: "One strike, one kill."

You may be saying to yourself right now: "What!!!! I thought this was supposed to be a book about nailing the job interview?" You're right. It is. I just wanted to open this chapter with an analogy because I thought, primarily, that it would be fun! Also, it does drive a point home: That in order to be good at this process you need to acquire knowledge, train yourself for the encounter, and build confidence through experience.

Does this make more sense now? I hope so. Now let's get into the meat of the interview process with some specific examples of questions you may be asked, and a demonstration of what the hiring managers are looking for.

I purposely do not give you any responses, but rather give more general principles as to how you may want to try and frame your answers.

I. Safety

Health and safety is a huge driver in todays world, as it should be, and you are most definitely going to see one of these questions in your work career as you interview for different jobs. Here are two examples as to how these questions might be framed.

Question: "*Can you tell us a time when you identified a possible safety issue? Can you tell us what it was, what you did about it, and what the outcome of your actions were?*"

"*Can you tell us a time when you maybe did something that*

wasn't safe? What was it, and how did you reflect on it afterward?"

When you answer questions such as these, as with all the questions, try and remember the best example you can and go with that. If you come up with an answer but you know it's not your best, then go with it anyway if that's the only one you can think of at the time. The hiring managers are really looking for your thought process more than just you being a superhero who saved someone's life!

Also, do you see how they can sometimes turn it around and fish for a negative experience? This is common as well because they want to see how you deal with bad situations, and if you can handle correction and learn from your mistakes.

II. Productivity

This kind of question is presented more in a manufacturing environment than anywhere else, but it can crop up in office jobs as well. For example: If you are looking to secure a position in a busy law firm this could be one of the questions you are asked. Productivity is important when you have constant deadlines to meet with your clients; particularly when you work for a real-estate lawyer who is always closing deals, etc.

Question: *"Can you tell us a time when you were really under the gun and you just felt that you had too much work to do? What were the specifics of the situation, what did you do, and what was the result of your actions?"*

"Can you tell us a time when you improved your productivity beyond what you previously thought was possible?"

Remember also, that if you don't have much work experience with something like productivity you can always pull examples from home life and school. For example: Maybe you needed to study for three exams and you were also slotted to help your buddies win the big baseball tournament? How did you manage to cram all that work into a short time and be successful (or mostly successful)? It's ok to think beyond work.

III. Quality

Quality is another big factor! I don't know about you, but I don't like purchasing poor workmanship! Now, I need to qualify that a bit. If you pay a really low price for a product or service that would otherwise cost far more, unless you're getting an exceptional deal, you may not want to gear yourself up to expect the best quality. On the other hand, if the product or service is definitely worth the price, you should *expect* exceptional quality! When my wife and I bought our third home we really had our heart set on a Miele dishwasher because we have a large family and these are reported to be the best on the market for the amount of use we were going to put through it. The catch was that we had to pay more (close to twice as much), which we did, because we felt it was worth the cost. We have never regretted our decision. And no, I was not paid a cent to "advertise" here for Miele! I just wanted to share a personal reflection that I'm sure many of you can relate to.

Question: "*Have you ever experienced a time when the quality of work you, or another member of your team, were producing was not up to what it should be? What was the issue, what did you do about it, and what was the result?*"

This next question doesn't follow the same pattern of behaviour based interviewing, but I have heard it a lot so you should be prepared to speak to it.

"*What does quality mean to you?*"

This is really broad, but I think most hiring managers really just want to know what your understanding of quality is. I have heard a lot of explanations as to what this means to people, and everything I have heard was pretty decent. It's more of a "gut-check" question around comprehension or understanding. There is really no wrong answer to this question, but some answers are definitely better than others, so you may want to give this question some thought during your interview prep time.

IV. Working with people of other ethnicities

There is no doubt today that, particularly in North America, we are working with people who come from literally all over the globe! Most of them come here in order to improve their lives or give their children more opportunity than they would have back in their own country. My next door neighbours who are from England are an example of this very thing. I would also like to state that, in my experience, most are honest hardworking people who appreciate what Canada and the US have to offer. Sure, there are definitely those few who do come here wanting to change our laws (particularly in Canada) to match those of the countries from which they left, and to abuse and leach off the system because they see us as too weak to do anything about it. Many of our politicians give in and cater to these whiners because they don't have the courage to stand up for what's right and protect our citizens and those immigrants who truly want to contribute to our society! Get this: Some of them leave their own countries and try to declare their rights to impose upon our society (or even their groups within our society) their laws (such as Sharia Law which they tried to get accepted in Ontario!) even though these are the very laws that helped to contribute to the oppression of their own county! The logical fallacies of these actions are hard to fathom! I'm not saying that we don't have room for improvement in our country, but I would question why people who think and act like this are even here.

Enough of that sidetrack! Let's focus again on the question at hand.

Question: *"Tell us about a situation where you had to work with someone from a different cultural background."*

Again, this can be a work situation, which is always preferable, or perhaps an encounter outside of work. It's pretty easy to come up with some example of encountering others from a different ethnicity in todays world. Your response also doesn't need to be a negative situation that turned positive; it can also be generally a positive one where you learned how better to deal with someone from a different culture by that person better instructing you through a personal relationship, or you doing some research, etc. I'm sure that if you think about it there was a time when you were face to face with someone not from Canada or the US, and they didn't even try to act like they were. I actually find different cultures interesting as it helps me to better deal with people in a positive way.

V. Conflict resolution

Dun ... Dun ... Dun!!!!! This is the big question that everyone wants to know about! Let me be blunt on this one. I would rather hire a person who can do the job but may have less aptitude, smarts, or whatever you want to call it, then someone who is brilliant but a complete jerk! As long as the person with the better attitude can make the cut and be successful, she will have my vote any day of the week over the arrogant, cocky, train wreck who enjoys creating and being a part of the drama that turns peoples lives upside-down! That's just me. I wager, however, that I'm not alone in this assessment.

Question: *"Over the course of our lives we all experience conflict at one time or other. Can you give us an example of a time you had a disagreement or argument with a boss, co-worker,*

*friend, or family member? What was the disagreement or argu-
ment about, how did you solve it (if you did), and what was the
result of your resolution; what did you learn?"*

If we are honest with ourselves we will admit that we are
sometimes at fault for at least portions of the arguments we
engage in. There is usually some blame on all sides, and
most hiring managers like it when people are honest and
admit that they were probably at fault in some of what
happened. It shows a great deal of maturity when you can
honestly try to see the other person's side. You still might
not agree, but at least you are able to show that you understand why they were upset. Now, with that said, there are
some arguments where one party is totally off-base and the
disagreement needs to be dealt with. These are also good
examples which can be used in an interview, particularly if
the argument stemmed from a health and safety issue, or
that of well-being (mental or otherwise). I need to caution
you, however, that you need to be careful how you present
the circumstance. Some people just come off mean and
negative when explaining a sharp disagreement as it still
might get their blood boiling! You need to ensure that this
does not happen! Objectivity is the best path, if it is possible
for you.

VI. Process

This question appears more often than not in an interview for some sort of manufacturing job, but it might just
show up in other areas as well. You need to be ready for
anything!

*Question: "Can you remember a time when you were
working on a project or with a team and you were able to develop
a new process, or you realized that the process you were working
with wasn't working? What was the situation, what did you do
about it, and what was the outcome?"*

As I mentioned above a few times: you can use examples from any area of life. For this one, for example, if you are fresh out of school, maybe it was a new method of studying that allowed you to get higher grades with substantially less effort. This maybe allowed you to get more work done elsewhere, or something like that. Again, be truthful and don't use this example unless it has actually happened to you! I just wanted to illustrate how broad you can pull your experience from.

VII. Work Teams

Despite the fact that some people prefer to be left alone (I believe that this number is actually minuscule compared to the rest of humanity!) we are creatures of social nature, and need to be together in some form or other. This includes having to work together. I once heard it said that you can choose who you hang out with but you can't choose who you work with! In reality, that choice is made by the people who are sitting across from you in the interview! Almost every work environment places you with a team of people who are there for a common purpose, aim, or objective. Therefore, we need to know how to work effectively within a group which is why hiring managers and HR ask these types of questions.

Question: "*Can you tell us a time when you worked within a dysfunctional team? What were the challenges, and were you able to overcome them fully or to some degree in order to be productive?*"

Here's another example as to how this style of question might be asked.

"*Can you tell us when you worked with, what you would consider, the best team environment you have ever experienced?*"

The idea here is for the managers and HR to understand what kind of team experiences you have had, and how you handled them: the good and the bad.

VIII. Leadership

The next ones we are going to talk about are the leadership questions. These are typically only in those interviews where the hiring managers are looking for someone with leadership ability, experience, or both. Sometimes it might be a requirement of the job which, therefore, makes these questions key.

Now, I just want to set the record straight and tell you that not everyone is supposed to be, or has the ability to be, in a leadership position! Does this shock you? You might say no. Then again, you might say yes, because you might have been told that you can't just stay in the position you enjoy doing and are good at, but you need to develop and move up to a leadership role. I have had this discussion with a few managers in my time saying that not everyone wants to move up, and that's ok.

Maybe we should let Bob be the best assembler he can be because he loves it and is good at it! Some people get sidetracked with the modern way of thinking that everyone can be whatever they want to be. That's not true! Some people either lack the ability, training, or opportunity for certain jobs. That's not to say that if someone wants to excel and put themselves out there for a certain position that they shouldn't go for it. All I'm saying is that some people aren't geared for certain jobs, and they may not have the opportunities to obtain those positions.

Let's take a few examples. For instance, if you're honest, you have to admit that there are some people who are big name actors today that are terrible, but there they are, making way more than you or I! How did that happen? It happened mainly because they were in the right place, at the right time, with maybe the right look. You then may see others who are fantastic actors doing any side acting job they can because they have yet to be that guy or girl who is there at the right time.

My son Joshua is another example. He has high functioning Asperger's and doesn't do well in high stress situations which makes him a non- candidate for any sort of emergency services work. Furthermore, does everyone have the ability, aptitude, skill-set, or opportunity to become an astronaut? There are innumerable examples that I can reference to further prove my point, yet the whole world says that you can do whatever you want!

Now, just to clarify, there are some amazing people out there who have overcome some huge obstacles and they ought to be commended, but that is not the normal way things work, unfortunately. My personal view is that we need to be able to recognize the doors of opportunity when they arise and go for those higher positions if we want them, but understand that it's ok to be the best at what you do, where you are, if it makes you content. I'm not going to stop pursuing certain things I want to accomplish in life, but I may have to sit back from time to time and take a realistic look at some of my goals. It's called self-reflection. If you want to go for the stars and you have the door before you, or you have a way to open the door, then by all means give it your best!

Now that I'm done with that rabbit trail, let's continue.

Question: "*What kind of leader do you consider yourself.*"

"*Can you give us an example of how you have led a team or group in the past?*"

"*In your view, what is the toughest part about being a leader? Can you give us an example as to how you have overcome that?*"

This is a pretty broad category and the questions could go on for a long time. I think, however, that you get the idea.

IX. The Animal Question

Finally, the animal question. I was talking about this book with a very good friend of mine who is an HR professional and she asked if I had included the animal question? Jillian went on to explain that it is becoming very popular in HR circles these days and that she uses it on every single interview she does. This was very intriguing to me as I had never heard of, or experienced, this question before, so I asked her to explain it to me. After she did I thought that it was an interesting way to potentially reveal some characteristics of a person. It can obviously be misleading, but I would wager to guess that it probably works in some cases. Warning: you may find it flakey but hey, let's include it here anyway just for fun.

Question: *"If you could be any type of animal, what would it be and why?"*

There you have it! The animal question, or, as I recently termed it: "The 'wild' truth!" Before you answer this one, you should give it some thought. Be honest as always, but sometimes it may hurt you if you don't qualify your answer. What do I mean by that you ask? I mean that there are some animals that people choose that may not be the most flattering, or demonstrate the abilities they would want demonstrated! Here are some examples:

Cat: Jillian had this answer once and the way the person framed it guaranteed that the candidate was not going to get the job! She said she wanted to be a cat because they sleep most of the day and lay around for the rest! Not a bright cookie that one!

Cats are fine, but you need to qualify it. For example, there are other cat qualities that would be great to possess;

try focussing on those. As you noticed, I am purposely not giving you exact examples of answers as I believe you need to work these questions out for yourself. That is the only way you will get good at this process!

Sloth: I'm pretty sure this one is self- explanatory! If you're not sure what I mean, just watch the movie "Zootopia" and you will find out!

Skunk: Again, probably not the best choice, but you may have a better idea than me about qualifying this one! Give it a shot at your own risk if you want!

Badger: This one might be ok if you qualify it properly but, in general, badgers are jerks!

Racoon: Really!!!! You're going to pick an animal that is known for thievery! It's up to you, but good luck!

Ostridge: I don't think anyone would ever pick this, but you never know in our twisted world these days! Let's take a better look at this creature. Contrary to popular belief, this bird does not put its head in the sand in order to "avoid" danger. However, from a distance, it does appear that it is doing just that when it is digging a nest, turning its eggs, or scavenging for food. The appearance of what it is doing is not great, and most people still believe the myth of "putting its head into the sand" and you may have a hard time explaining this. Its redeeming quality is that this animal is fast! They even race these in certain parts of the world!

I think this list could definitely go on and on and on! The point is that you better have a good reason why you are choosing the animal you are, and you should try and stay away from one that has qualities that are less than savoury! In all honesty, you may never be asked this question. If you are, however, wouldn't it be great if you had an answer ready? As a friend of mine used to say back in the day when we played RPG's (Role Playing Games; the actual book, pen, and paper ones!): "The choice is yours, but choose wisely!"

The Conclusion to the Matter

I hope that this chapter has given you a better idea and understanding about the reason for, and the format of, the types of questions that can be asked in the interview process. This list was merely an example of what might be asked as there are multitudes of other areas which are important to those who are looking to bring on new employees.

As a point of advice: As I mentioned earlier (it's that important that I restate it!), if you are asked a vague and broad question that doesn't fit with this "Situation Task Action Result" format, then answer it in that way anyway. If you do, you will absolutely sound like a genius! You will be the rock star of interviews! They will literally be blown away!

Happy hunting!

7

THE LAST QUESTION

I didn't realize just how ominous the title to this chapter was until I wrote it down and looked at it for a moment! Don't worry, it's not the last question you will ever be asked, unless of course you have a tragic incident occur after the interview which is incredibly unlikely!

Moving on now, I would like to say that there is, in most interviews, one final question which is always asked of the prospective candidate. This question brings everything to a summation and indicates where your thought process is for the future. This question may be a little different from the rest in that there is not really a wrong way to answer it; it completely depends on what the hiring managers and HR are looking for and how much flexibility they will allow in the answer. I have heard some people give answers to this question that I personally didn't think were very good, but some of the other managers who were with me liked those answers!

IN SAYING THAT, I would like to add that there are some

general principles which can be used in order to help frame your answer in such a way that it gives you the best possible chance of striking a chord with the hiring team.

Before revealing it, I would also like to add that there can be two questions that are tied together. Again, I am speaking from my experience as I am sure there are tons of renditions of how these interviews close. This is what I used, and what many others who interviewed me used.

Now that I have you all psyched up for it, here it is!

Question: "*Do you have any questions for us?*"

What! You shout! You built me up for this, a reverse question! Yes ... yes I did. This question may, at first glance, look simple, but don't let the looks deceive you! Hidden deep down in the recesses of the plain looking letters which make up the simple words is a lurking, probing spirit waiting to devour your very soul! Whoa! Way too dramatic! Maybe. But that's the way I roll!

Listen, the intent of this question is for you to show more interest in the position, or company, in an intellectual way. What do you mean by that you ask? Well, why don't I show you by giving you an example.

Years ago, after I got my Emergency Medical Technician - Ambulance (EMT-A) registration from the province of Alberta, I was interviewed for a job with the City of Calgary. At the end of this interview they asked me this question and I answered it roughly in this way:

"Yes. The question I have for you is, 'If I am the successful candidate for this position, what other opportunities, and or positions, are available for me as I pursue my career as an EMT? Where can I go with the city of Calgary to further my career?'"

Do you get the idea? This is solid and shows that you desire to grow in your selected field. Management loves that! Remember, however, be honest! If it's not your intent to advance beyond the selected job, then try to frame this in as positive a light as you can. For example, you can ask what level of proficiency is available for you in the current position. Or, you can ask if there is opportunity to move laterally into different positions via cross training etc. Just give it some thought so you don't go charging into the interview half-cocked, and look like a deer in headlights when this question comes up. And yes, I was offered the job, but kindly declined it as I had a young family at the time and the transition to shift work gave me "cold feet."

Just so you know, in my experience, not having a question to ask them is almost as bad as asking a stupid one!

8

THE CONCLUDING IMPRESSION

Remember way back at the beginning of this literary adventure where I mentioned that first impressions are incredibly important? Well so are concluding impressions! You need to show the individual, or team, who is looking at hiring you that you are consistent from start to finish. This is also the time that, if you made a bad first impression for whatever reason (lack of coffee, lack of sleep, nervousness, stress, etc.), you have an opportunity to correct it.

I get it. Sometimes we're not always on our game are we? I don't know how many times I have met someone for the first time and said or did something that I consider stupid. Like the time I was invited to our friend's brand new house for a celebration. You see, they are from Nigeria and I guess in Nigeria getting into a new home is a huge event that involves multitudes of friends and family. And yes, our friends, being from Nigeria, are black (trust me this is important). While I was mingling and meeting people I shook hands with another white guy and introduced myself. Then I asked if he was a friend or part of the family! He looked at me kind of stunned at first and then said flatly, "Friend." I didn't think about how stupid that sounded until I had time to reflect on it later. When I originally asked the question, what I really wanted to ask is was he a friend or *married* into the family, but I didn't. That would have made more sense, but instead he is one of those guys out there that now has a story to tell about a guy he met who he now thinks is an idiot.

I'm sure there are many more people out there wondering if I'm functionally retarded! I can either laugh at it or cry and I choose to laugh. I learned a long time ago that I can't take myself too seriously! It's because I can relate so well with embarrassing experiences that causes me to, when I watch a movie where a character is doing something incredibly embarrassing, hide my face in a pillow and scream, "NOOOOOOO!!!!!!!!!" I feel for them!

Back to the point. Remember to thank them for their time and consideration, give them a firm handshake, smile, and you're done. It's that simple! If, however, you are an introvert, and this sort of thing challenges you, then you need to, as I mentioned earlier in the book, practice these simple skills in order to ensure that they don't hinder you. Human's, however, are unpredictable sometimes and the best techniques still may not land you the job, but what I have shown you here will definitely appeal to the broadest cross-section of people which will give you the greatest chance of nailing the interview.

I really hope this helps!

9

THE WRAP UP

As we have seen throughout this book, it's easier than people think for you to nail the interview process! Too many people stress out about it needlessly. The reason they do, I am convinced, is because they don't know the reason for the method, or the right way to apply themselves to the process. In short: they are not prepared.

Here are the keys which I hope have armed you with a better appreciation for the job interview, as well as the tools you need to unlock this process for yourself and help you be successful.

#1: First Impressions

#2: The Question Style ("STAR" Situation, Task, Action, Result)

#3: How to Answer

#4: Specific Examples

#5: The "Last" Question

#6: The Concluding Impression

Before I leave you to apply these keys, I would like to

show you how Joe's interview would have gone had he known what you have just learned and applied it himself.

JOE WALKED CONFIDENTLY up the long path that led to the front of a large brown building. Over the door was a sign which said, "Smith Brothers." Joe had been trying to get a job interview with the Smith Brothers machining company for a long time and now his day had come!

He checked his watch and saw that he was about ten minutes early for his appointment. *Perfect!* He thought to himself as he opened the glass door that led to the front office area. Once inside, he strode up to the front desk and greeted the secretary warmly. "Hi," he said with a slight smile. "I'm scheduled for a job interview at ten."

The secretary smiled back and said, "Ok. Your name is ... "

"Joe," he responded.

"Great Joe. I'll let them know you're here. You can have a seat in the lobby and someone will come out and get you momentarily."

"Excellent. Thanks!" Joe responded as he took a seat in the lobby.

After a few moments Joe noticed an older man, sharply dressed, walking toward him. The man smiled as Joe rose up and held out his hand. "I'm Don," he said.

Joe smiled back and grasped Don's hand firmly. "It's nice to meet you," he said politely. "I'm Joe."

Don smiled back and said, "Please come this way,"

The two walked down a short corridor and turned into the second doorway on the right. As they strolled down the hallway and into the room Joe asked Don how his day was and made some light small-talk. The room they entered was well lit with a large oval table positioned in the centre. As they entered, Joe noticed two other people sitting at the table: a short stocky man with a round face, and a younger woman with shoulder length blonde hair. They both greeted him with smiles, handshakes, and introductions. The man's name was Devon, and the woman's was Jennifer.

After everyone was seated Devon asked Joe how we was doing today.

"Pretty good," replied Joe, looking Devon in the eyes with a big smile.

"That's great!" Devon responded with a smile of his own. "Now, I just want to let you know at the outset that we have allotted 30 minutes for the interview. We have a number of what we call 'behavioural event' questions, where we will ask for specific examples as to a time you have demonstrated a certain behaviour. Please try and be as specific as you can. We will all be asking questions and all of us will be taking notes. Don't be alarmed; it's for our benefit so we can remember how each candidate answers the particular question. We have bad memories." Devon smiled and chuckled as he ended.

Joe smiled back, completely at ease with this type of interview. "Sounds good," he replied. "Ok Joe," began Jennifer. "Can you please tell us a little bit about your previous work history ... say ... for the last 5 years?"

Joe leaned forward in his chair and began to easily recite his work history. He looked around at each member of the hiring team as he did so, ensuring that he made eye contact with each person as he spoke. His work history was actually really good, but the display of his confidence as he recited it was even better!

After he was done, Devon took the lead and asked the

first question: "Who do you think is responsible for safety in the workplace, and why?"

"Well, in my experience, the primary person responsible for safety in the workplace is myself and every individual employee. We need to first take care of ourselves. If everyone is doing that, then the culture of safety will be part of everything we do. After that, on a higher level, it's members of the safety committee, the Health and Safety Manager, and the rest of the Leadership team," Joe replied.

"On the same topic," Don interjected, "can you tell us if you have ever seen a safety violation, and, if so what did you do about that?"

Joe thought for a second and then said, "Actually, in my last job there were a number of safety issues which I brought up and helped to resolve, but the most notable one that I can think of right now was when I noticed that the product we were building continued to get heavier and heavier as the marketing people were doing everything they could to cram as many components into the units as possible because that is what the customers are asking for. I started getting concerned about this because I wasn't sure our forklifts on the shipping dock were rated to lift so much weight. So I went and read the plate on one of the trucks, got a shipper to help me weigh the product, and cross- referenced the numbers. Sure enough, the product had become overweight and we needed to find a different way of lifting it. I brought this to the attention of Health and Safety and the Management team who began to quickly source a resolution."

"What eventually happened?" Jennifer asked.

"We had to lease two new trucks which were specific for shipping and receiving in order to handle the loads."

Jennifer smiled and began to write more notes. The

interview went on through question after question, and Joe was able to come up with answers for all of it from the experiences he accumulated in his personal and professional life. The interview went slightly over the allotted time, but the hiring team didn't seem to mind.

After it was finished, Don, Devon, and Jennifer gave Joe a warm goodbye and said they would be in touch with him in about a week. Joe walked out of the interview confident that he had given it his best and knew he had a decent shot at winning the job!

There you go! Now it's your turn! Go ahead and ROCK IT!

ABOUT THE AUTHOR

Chad Stewart is an accomplished teacher and author. He looks for opportunities to use his teaching skill to instruct in every area he has knowledge in. The fields are broad and encompass leadership, interviewing, emergency medicine, firefighting, biblical theology, life skills, and such. One of his greatest feelings of his accomplishments is seeing "the lights come on" in those whom he is able to pass knowledge onto. Despite all the teaching he is involved in, he remains a student at heart and in practice. He believes that there is always something more to learn and to pass on to others.

Made in the USA
Columbia, SC
05 March 2018